Table of Contents

General Instructions

Choosing Fabric

Choosing fabric for a project can be the most enjoyable part of the whole process. Don't be afraid of this step! Start with one fabric you really like and pull the coordinating colors from it. Or, even easier, use one of those coordinated fat quarter bundles you have purchased. Those fabrics have been selected by experts in the quilt shop, or may be part or all of a fabric collection, in which case the fabrics are designed to work together!

You can choose the same fabrics for a small quilt that you would pick for a large quilt. The scale of the design does not have to be small. Choose a large design if it looks good cut into smaller pieces. Also choose a larger print for the border or large units in the quilt such as alternate blocks. If in doubt, make up one block before cutting the whole project.

Preparation

You may choose to pre-wash your fabrics or not. They lose some of their body when you wash them, and you may have some loss with raveling. A little spray starch or sizing can restore the body. If you are eager to start a new project, you can simply pretest for color bleeding by spritzing a small area of the fabric with water, placing a white fabric over it, then ironing. If you get color transfer, perhaps you'd better pre-wash.

Ironing the folds out of the fabrics before cutting is a necessary step for accurate cutting.

Cutting

Accuracy is always important in the cutting process, but even more so with little quilts; there is less room for error. Also, the pieces will fit together more readily if you've taken the time to cut them accurately. Some tips for accurate cutting:

* Work in good light, daylight if possible.

* Iron the fabrics before cutting.

* Cut only two layers of fabric at a time. Any time you save in cutting more layers will be lost when the pieces don't fit accurately.

* Keep your tools from slipping; use the film or sandpaper that adheres to the backside of the tools.

* Use a sharp rotary cutter and a good mat. Mats do wear out after a time, as too many grooves get cut into them. Replace blades and mats as needed; this is not an area to cut corners (no pun intended!).

Sewing

Quarter-inch seams are so important! If at all possible, find a ¼" (6mm) foot for your sewing machine. They are well worth the small investment.
  If you have problems with mad feed dogs chewing up your fabric, try these tricks to tame them:

* Insert a new needle, preferably a smaller one.

* Clean your sewing machine, particularly the fuzz under the throat plate.

* Consider switching to a single-hole throat plate (instead of the wide opening for zigzag).

* Chain-sew whenever possible.

* Begin and end with a scrap of fabric, an "engine" and "caboose."

Un-sewing

It's a fact of life, sometimes we make mistakes or the pieces don't fit properly. Fortunately, the seams on little quilts are short and the pieces small, so any un-sewing goes quickly. However, don't get hung up on perfection. Fix the areas that bother you (learn from your mistakes!) and move on to the next step.

Pressing

Remember the purpose of pressing is to make the seam/unit/block/quilt FLAT. Keep that thought in mind while pressing. I prefer to iron from the right side whenever possible. Pressing arrows are given in the diagrams. If you use these, most, if not all, of your seams will alternate.

TIPS:

Try this quick check to see if you are sewing an exact ¼" (6mm) seam: Cut three $1\frac{1}{2}$" × $3\frac{1}{2}$" (3.8cm × 8.9cm) strips. Sew them together on the long edges. Press. The square should now measure $3\frac{1}{2}$" (8.9cm). If not, adjust your seam allowance. (Also, check that you have pressed correctly.)

Twisting the Seam

Try this neat trick whenever piecing any type of four-patch unit. It will make the center intersection lie flatter.

1. Before pressing the last seam on a four-patch, grasp the seam with both hands about an inch (2.5cm) from the center seam. Twist in opposite directions, opening up a few threads in the seam.

2. Press one seam one direction, the other seam the opposite direction. In the center you will see a tiny four-patch appear, and the center now lays flat.

Borders

We often make this more difficult than it needs to be. Simply cut the strips designated for the borders, place them on top of the quilt, measuring through the middle of the quilt. Measure for the borders with the fabric strips themselves. Always measure with two strips at a time so the borders are guaranteed to be the same length! I crease the border at the proper length, and cut a bit longer for insurance. Pin the borders to the quilt and sew.

Mitered Borders

Occasionally, to look best, borders need to be mitered. To cut mitered borders, add the width of two extra borders to the length. Also, add a couple of inches for "insurance." For example: the quilt top measures 20" × 30" (50.8cm × 76.2cm) and you are adding 3" (7.6cm) wide borders. For the top and bottom of the quilt you would cut 20" + 3" + 3" + 2" (insurance) = 28" (50.8cm + 7.6cm + 7.6cm + 5.1cm = 71.1cm). For the sides, 30" + 3" + 3" + 2" = 38" (76.2cm + 7.6cm + 7.6cm + 5.1cm = 96.5cm).

1. Find the center of each border and the center of the corresponding edge of the quilt. Pin together in the center. Sew the borders to the quilt, stopping and backstitching ¼" (6mm) from the corner of the quilt.

2. Fold the quilt on the diagonal, with right sides together, matching raw edges of the borders. The borders will extend outward.

3. Place the Companion Angle (or a ruler) on your quilt with the longest edge on the diagonal of the quilt, and a 45-degree line (or the edge of the Companion Angle) aligned with the raw edges of the borders.

4. Draw a diagonal line from the end of the stitching line to the raw edges of the border.

5. Pin the borders together along this marked line. Sew on the line, backstitching at the inside corner.

6. Check the seam on the right side. If it lies flat, without tucks or pleats, trim the seam to ¼" (6mm). Press open or to one side. Repeat on all 4 corners.

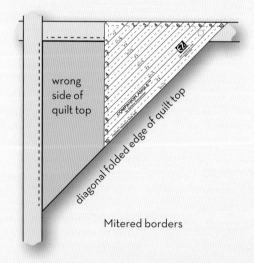

Mitered borders

Batting Choices

The small quilts look (and hang) best with a lightweight flat batting. A good choice is a lightweight cotton, or Thermore by Hobbs Bonded Fibers (a lightweight polyester batting designed for garments).

Quilting

Small quilts generally don't require lots of quilting, and easily can be machine quilted. They also are ideal take-along hand quilting projects! Quilting suggestions are given with each project. Choose to quilt them as I have done, or experiment with your own technique. This is the perfect place to try that new thread or technique.

Binding

When the quilting is complete, baste a scant ¼" (6mm) around the perimeter of the quilt. This will prevent the layers from shifting while the binding is being sewn on.

1. Cut the binding strips either bias or straight-of-grain, single or double. The pattern will recommend a size and type, but the final choice is up to you! For these little quilts a single-fold binding is sufficient. Bias or straight-of-grain bindings work equally well on a straight edge. You MUST use a bias binding on scalloped or curved edges.

2. To cut bias strips, align the 45-degree line on your ruler on the left edge of your fabric. Cut on the diagonal in the width chosen for the quilt.

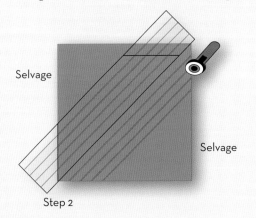

Selvage

Selvage

Step 2

3. Join all binding strips with diagonal seams pressed open. For a double binding, fold in half the long way, and press with wrong sides together.

4. Sew the binding to the quilt with a ¼" (6mm) seam, mitering the corners. To miter, sew within a ¼" (6mm) from the corner (or the width of your seam allowance). Stop and backstitch. Remove the quilt from under the presser foot, and clip the threads.

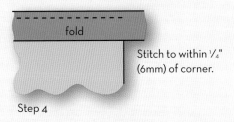

fold

Stitch to within ¼" (6mm) of corner.

Step 4

5. Fold the binding straight up and straight back down, aligning with the next edge to be sewn.

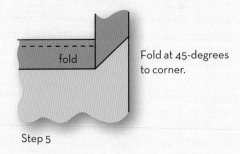

fold

Fold at 45-degrees to corner.

Step 5

6. Begin stitching at the fold. Repeat in this manner around the quilt.

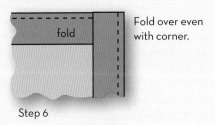

fold

Fold over even with corner.

Step 6

Quilt Labels

Your quilts are your legacy, so sign them! An artist would sign on the front, but you may want to add more information to your quilt. A label should include the following information:

- Quilt recipient
- Quilt maker (and possibly the quilter if not yourself)
- Date of completion/presentation
- Where it was made (city, country)
- Special occasion or story

You can purchase a fabric label to write on or create your own. Sew or appliqué the label to the quilt either before or after the quilt is completed.

Washing and Storing

With reasonable care a quilt can last for many generations. Remember to protect the quilt from light, smoke, pets, small children, high heat and humidity.

Store in a pillowcase, never in plastic, paper or against wood. Try to store flat if possible.

If washing is necessary, use one of the detergents made specifically for washing quilts. Wash the quilt in lukewarm water. If stains need to be removed, soak in a solution of OxiClean for up to three days. Do not agitate in the washing machine, but wash gently by hand. You can spin out a quilt in the washing machine to remove the excess water. Rinse in the same manner.

To dry, lay flat with a fan blowing over the quilt. Turn over and dry the backside the same way. Allow the quilt to dry thoroughly before storing. With loving care, your quilts can become treasured heirlooms for generations to come.

Tri-Recs™ Tools Tutorial

To cut Tri triangles, lay the tool on the strip with the top flat edge at the top of the strip and a line on the tool aligned with the bottom of the strip. Cut on both sides of the triangle. The patterns will tell you what size strip to cut—always ½" (1.3cm) larger than the finished size.

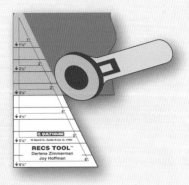

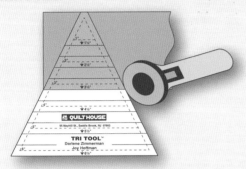

For the second cut, rotate the tool so it is pointing down. Align as before and cut.

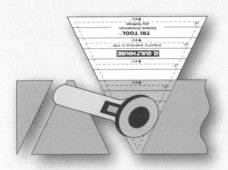

To cut Recs triangles, cut the same size strip as for the large triangles. Leave the strip folded and you will automatically cut pairs of Recs triangles. Align the tool with the flat top edge at the top of the strip, and a line on the tool aligned with the bottom of the strip. Cut on the angled edge, then swing around and nip off the "magic angle" at the top. This needs to be cut accurately, as it is your alignment guide when sewing the pieces together.

For the second cut, rotate the tool so it is pointing down. Align as before and cut, then swing back and trim off the "magic angle."

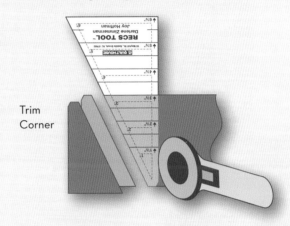

Trim Corner

Together the two tools cut the shapes for making a triangle within a square. Lay out the pieces as shown to form a square.

Fit the Recs triangle into the corner of the large triangle. Note how the "magic angle" will fit right into the corner as shown. Yes, the pieces look odd at this point, but they will be right when sewn!

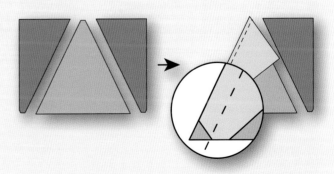

Vintage Baby Quilt

This little quilt is NOT a vintage baby quilt, but made to look like one. I had an extra pieced strip from a larger vintage strippy quilt, and I recycled it into this little quilt. Basically, it is made up of nine-patches sewn together into long strips. The nine-patches were hand sewn, and are not terribly accurate. I did not try to "fix" the strips, but rather left them as they were, added the sashes and narrow border, and finished it.

If you want your little quilt to have an authentic vintage look, try piecing and quilting with less accuracy than usual. Take a casual approach! I also used a lightweight, soft batting (flannel can be used) and washed the quilt a number of times after completing to give it the patina of age.

MATERIALS

Fabric Requirements

- ⅜ yd (34.3cm) indigo print (sashes, border, binding)
- 6 fat quarters of assorted prints*
- ⅝ yd (57.1cm) backing
- 22" × 26" (55.9cm × 66cm) batting

*Note: For an authentic look, use reproduction indigos, gray (mourning) prints, woven plaids, stripes, a few old browns, double-pinks and burgundy-red prints.

TIP:

Occasionally you can find a set of vintage four-patch or nine-patch blocks; these could be used with this pattern to make up a "vintage" doll or baby quilt.

CUTTING DIRECTIONS

Materials	Cut	To Yield
From each fat quarter	(3) 2" × 15" (5.1cm × 38.1) strips	Strip sets
Indigo print	(3) 2" × 40" (5.1cm × 1m) strips (3) 2" × 40" (5.1cm × 1m) strips	Vertical sashes, borders Binding

Sew exact ¼" (6mm) seams throughout. Place fabrics right sides together for sewing, unless otherwise noted.

Assemble the Strip Sets

(Make 6)

1. Sew together 3 different 2" × 15" (5.1cm × 38.1cm) print strips to make a strip set. Press the seams all 1 direction. Repeat for the remainder of the 2" × 15" (5.1cm × 38.1cm) strips (Figure 1).

Figure 1

2. Cut each of the strip sets into seven 2" (5.1cm) wide units. You will have 42 units (Figure 2).

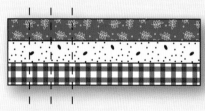

Figure 2

3. Sew 13 of these units together to form a strip, alternating the seams in each row. Press the seams all one direction. Make 3 rows of 13 units. You will have some units left over (Figure 3).

4. Measure, cut and sew the indigo sashing between the pieced rows from Step 3. Press toward the sashing.

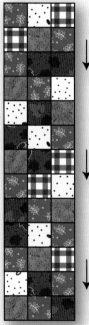

Figure 3

Borders

1. Measure, cut and sew 2 borders the width of the quilt. Sew to the top and bottom of the quilt. Press toward the borders.

2. In the same manner, measure, cut and sew borders to the sides of the quilt. Press.

Quilting Suggestions

To prepare the quilt for quilting, layer the backing (which has been cut at least 4" (10.2cm) larger than the quilt top) wrong side up, followed by the batting (again, cut larger than the quilt top) and last, the quilt top, right side up. Thread or pin baste in a 4" (10.2cm) grid across the quilt. Quilt as desired.

The quilt shown was hand quilted in a diagonal grid over the pieced rows. A simple cable was quilted in all of the sashes and borders with a cream-colored thread.

Binding

1. Before binding, hand baste a scant ¼" (6mm) from the edge of the quilt to prevent the layers from shifting.

2. Join the binding strips with diagonal seams pressed open. Press the binding in half lengthwise with wrong sides together.

3. Sew the binding to the quilt with a ¼" (6mm) seam. Trim excess batting and backing.

4. Turn the binding to the backside and stitch down by hand.

5. Sign and date your little quilt for the benefit of future quilt historians.

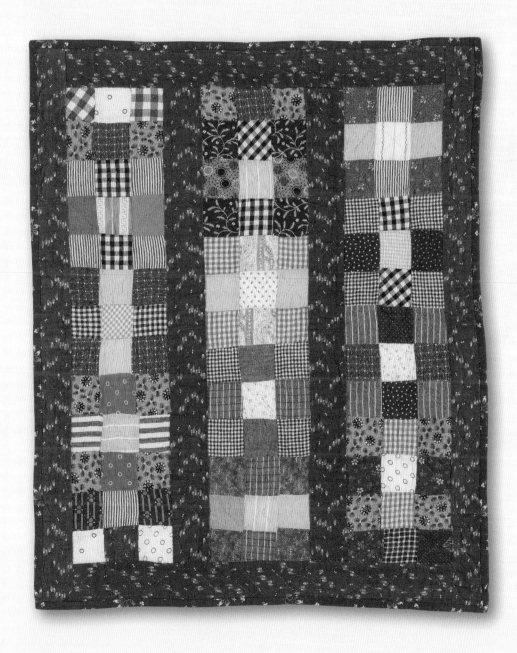

Quick-Trip Stroller Quilt

FINISHED DIMENSIONS: 34" × 38" (86.4CM × 96.5CM)   BLOCK SIZE: 2" (5.1CM)

Just right for the mom and baby on the go! Regular-sized baby quilts may be too large for a stroller or car seat, but this one is just right. No baby? Then sew a just-right blanket for a much loved pet. Don't be put off by all the small squares—this baby utilizes strip sets for easy cutting and piecing.

MATERIALS

Fabric Requirements
- fat quarters of each:
  - 1 yellow print
  - 3 blue prints
  - 2 green prints
  - 2 pink prints
  - 2 lavender prints
- green border and binding: ⅝ yd (57.7cm)
- backing: 1⅛ yd (93.7cm)
- batting: 38" × 42" (96.5cm × 1m)

CUTTING DIRECTIONS

Materials	Cut	To Yield
From each fat quarter	(4) 2½" × 21" (6.4cm × 53.3) strips	Strip sets

Arrange the colors as shown, or devise your own arrangement.

Assembling the Quilt

1. Sew the strips together into 2 different strip sets of 5 colors as shown (or your own arrangement of colors). Press the seams all one direction. Make 4 of each strip set for a total of 8 strip sets (Figure 1).

2. Cut a total of sixty-four 2½" (6.4cm) wide units. Sew the units together end to end as shown (Figure 2).

3. Sew the ends together to make 32 rings. Press these seams the same direction as the other seams (Figure 3).

4. Starting in the upper left corner of the quilt, remove 2 adjacent squares on one ring to make the first vertical row. Set aside the squares you have removed. Continue to remove squares from each ring using the diagram as a guide. You will need to re-press the seams in alternate rows to sew them together. Sew two of these sections exactly as shown. They will be the upper left and lower right sections of the quilt (Figure 4).

5. For the upper right and lower left sections of the quilt, piece 2 sections of the quilt according to the diagram at the right (Figure 5).

6. Using 2 more rings, sew together 2 vertical rows exactly as shown (Figure 6). Piece them between the upper 2 sections and the lower 2 sections. Press toward the center.

7. Using 2 more rings, sew together one horizontal row exactly as shown (Figure 7). Sew it between the upper and lower sections. Press away from the center.

8. From the green border print, cut four 2½" × 42" (6.4cm × 1m) strips. Measure across the width of the quilt. Trim 2 borders to this length and sew to the top and bottom of the quilt. Press the seams toward the borders. Repeat for the sides of the quilt.

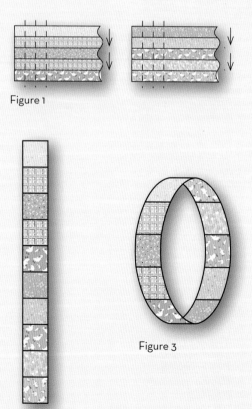

Figure 1

Figure 2

Figure 3

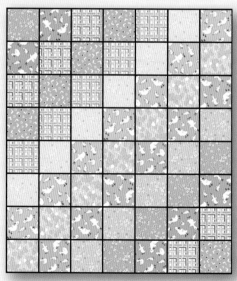

Figure 4

Finishing the Quilt

1. Layer the backing (wrong side up), the batting and the quilt top right side up. Baste and then quilt as desired.

2. From the green border print, cut four 2¼" × 42" (6.4cm × 1m) strips. Join with diagonal seams pressed open. Press the binding in half, right sides out, to make a double binding.

3. Before binding, hand-baste (or machine-baste using a walking foot) a scant ¼" (6mm) from the edge of the quilt to hold the layers together.

4. Sew the binding to the quilt with a ¼" (6mm) seam, mitering the corners and joining the ends. See General Instructions for more information.

5. Trim the excess batting and backing. Turn the binding to the back side and stitch down by hand with matching thread. Sign and date!

Figure 5

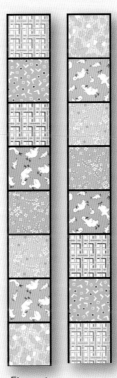

Figure 6

Figure 7

Gingham Flowers

FINISHED SIZE: 25½" × 33½" (64.6CM × 85CM) BLOCK SIZE: 3" (7.6CM)

There is something so delightful about gingham, even though woven or printed gingham fabrics have been around for more than 200 years. In this quilt, different colors of gingham "flowers" have been framed with a latticework of green print. The lattice is created with simple nine-patch blocks, and the two different blocks are set with sashing and cornerstones. What looks like a difficult quilt is indeed quite simple to make.

MATERIALS

Fabric Requirements

- ¾ yd (68.6cm) vintage white
- Fat quarters pink, blue, yellow and lavender gingham (or any four fabrics)
- ⅞ yd (80cm) green print
- ⅞ yd (80cm) backing
- 30" × 38" (76.2cm × 96.5cm) batting

Suggested Tool

- EZ Quilting Tri-Recs

Note: There is no substitute for the Tri-Recs tool.

CUTTING DIRECTIONS FOR FLOWER BLOCKS

Materials	Cut	To Yield
Vintage white	(4) 2" × 40" (5.1cm × 1m) strips	68 pairs of Recs* triangles
From 3 gingham fat quarters	(2) 2" × 20" (5.1cm × 50.8cm) strips	16 Tri triangles
From 1 gingham fat quarter	(2) 2" × 20" (5.1cm × 50.8cm) strips	20 Tri triangles

*Note: When cutting with the Recs tools, fold the strip in half and cut pairs. Don't forget to trim off the "magic angle." See General Instructions for details on using the Tri-Recs tool.

CUTTING DIRECTIONS FOR NINE-PATCH BLOCKS AND SASHING

Materials	Cut	To Yield
Vintage white	(4) 1½" × 40" (3.8cm × 1m) strips (6) 1½" × 40" (3.8cm × 1m) strips	Strip sets (58) 1½" × 3½" (3.8cm × 8.9cm) sashes
Green print	(5) 1½" × 40" (3.8cm × 1m) strips (6) 1½" × 40" (3.8cm × 1m) strips	Strip sets (24) 1½" (3.8cm) squares (cornerstones)

Sew exact ¼" (6mm) seams. Place fabrics right sides together for sewing, unless otherwise noted.

Assemble the Flower Blocks

(Make 17)

1. Open up the pairs of Recs triangles and place them on either side of the Tri triangles as shown (Figure 1). Sew a Recs triangle to the right side of the Tri triangle, fitting the "magic angle" into the corner (Figure 2). Press the seam toward the Recs triangle.

Figure 1

Figure 2
Make 68.

2. Sew a Recs triangle to the left side of the Tri-Recs units from Step 1. Press toward the triangle just added (Figure 3). At this point the unit should measure 2" (5.1cm) square.

Figure 3
Make 68.

3. Sew the Tri-Recs units from Step 2 together in matching pairs as shown (Figure 4). Press.

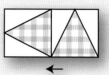

Figure 4
Make 34.

4. Sew matching pairs together to make flower blocks, matching and pinning at the intersection. Twist the seam where it intersects to open it (Figure 5). Press. Refer to General Instructions for more instruction on this technique. At this point the flower blocks should measure 3½" (8.9cm).

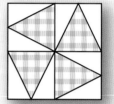

Figure 5
Make 17.

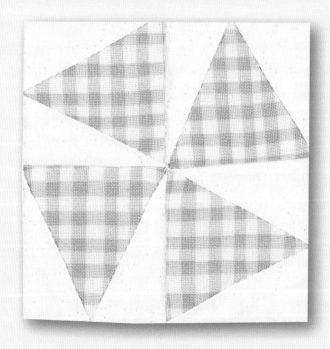

Assemble the Nine-Patch Blocks

(Make 18)

1. Sew together 2 strip sets of green, white, green. Press toward the green strips (Figure 6). At this point the strip sets should measure 3½" (8.9cm) wide. Cut into 36 units 1½" (3.8cm) wide.

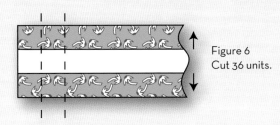

Figure 6
Cut 36 units.

3. Sew together 2 units from Step 1 and 1 unit from Step 2 to make a nine-patch block. Press. Make 18 blocks. At this point the blocks should measure 3½" (8.9cm) (Figure 8).

Figure 8
Make 18 blocks.

2. Sew together 1 strip set of white, green, white. Press toward the green strip. Cut into 18 units 1½" (3.8cm) wide (Figure 7).

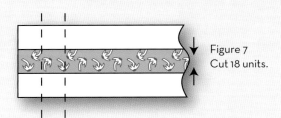

Figure 7
Cut 18 units.

Assemble the Quilt

1. Sew 4 white 1½" × 3½" (3.8cm × 8.9cm) sashing strips, 3 nine-patch blocks and 2 flower blocks together to make a row. Press toward the sashing strips. Make 4 rows (Figure 9).

2. Sew 4 white 1½" × 3½" (3.8cm × 8.9cm) sashing strips, 2 nine-patch blocks and 3 flower blocks together to make a row. Press toward the sashing strips. Make 3 rows (Figure 10).

3. Sew 5 white 1½" × 3½" (3.8cm × 8.9cm) sashes and 4 green cornerstones together to make a horizontal sashing row. Press toward the sashing strips. Make 6 rows (Figure 11).

4. Sew the Step 1, Step 2 and Step 3 rows together according to the Quilt Diagram. Press the seams toward the horizontal sashing rows.

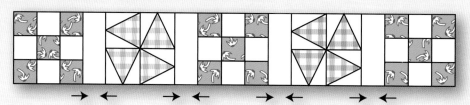

Figure 9
Make 4 rows.

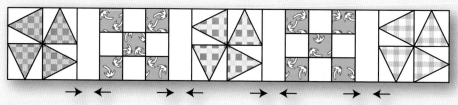

Figure 10
Make 3 rows.

Figure 11
Make 6 rows.

CUTTING DIRECTIONS FOR BORDERS AND BINDING

Materials	Cut	To Yield
Green print	(7) 1½" × 40" (3.8cm × 1m) strips (4) 2" (5.1cm) strips	Inner and outer borders Binding
From each gingham fat quarter	(2) 1½" × 20" (3.8cm × 50.8cm) strips	Strip sets

Borders

1. Measure, cut and sew a 1½" (3.8cm) green border to the top and bottom of the quilt. Press toward the border.

2. In the same manner, measure, cut and sew a 1½" (3.8cm) green border to the sides of the quilt. Press toward the border.

3. Sew the gingham strips together in this order: pink, blue, lavender and yellow. Press the seams all in 1 direction. Make 2 strip sets. Cut the strip sets into 26 units 1½" (3.8cm) wide (Figure 12).

4. Join 6 units from Step 3 to make the top border. Remove the last 3 squares. The border should begin and end with a pink square. Press. Make a second border just like this for the bottom of the quilt. Sew pieced borders to the top and bottom of the quilt. Press toward the green border (Figure 13).

5. Starting with the squares removed from the top and bottom borders, piece together eight units, including the partial unit from Step 4. The borders should have a yellow square on one end and a blue square on the other. Press seams all 1 direction. Make 2. Sew borders to the sides of the quilt. Press toward the green border (Figure 14).

6. In the same manner as in Steps 1 and 2, measure, cut and sew the green outer borders to the quilt. Press toward the borders just added.

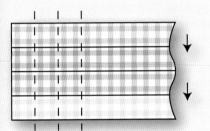

Figure 12

> **TIPS**
>
> If the pieced borders don't fit properly, take in or let out a few seams in the pieced border until it does fit.

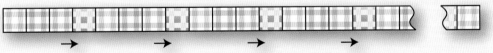

Figure 13

Figure 14

Quilting Suggestions

To prepare the quilt for quilting, layer the backing (which has been cut at least 4" (10.2cm) larger than the quilt top) wrong side up, followed by the batting (again, cut larger than the quilt top) and last, the quilt top, right side up. Thread or pin baste in a 4" (10.2cm) grid across the quilt. Quilt as desired.

The quilt shown was machine quilted in a meandering style in all the white areas. Straight lines, following the seam lines in the pieced borders, were hand quilted in the 3 borders.

Binding

1. Before binding, hand baste a scant ¼" (6mm) from the edge of the quilt. This will prevent the layers from shifting while the binding is being sewn on.

2. Join the binding ends with diagonal seams pressed open.

3. Press the binding in half lengthwise with wrong sides together.

4. Sew to the quilt with a ¼" (6mm) seam, mitering the corners.

5. Turn the binding to the backside and stitch down by hand with matching thread.

6. Sign and date your Gingham Flowers quilt!

Quilt Diagram

Sew-Easy Baby Quilt

FINISHED SIZE: 47" × 54½" (1.2M × 1.4M)   **BLOCK SIZE:** 7¾" (19.7CM)

This pattern really is sew easy! It's great for a beginning quilter or for someone who needs a quick baby gift. The block is simply a square framed with a contrasting color. The "piano key" border is made of rectangles—leftovers from the blocks. This border is very forgiving (if it doesn't fit properly, just take in or let out a few seams) and always coordinates with whatever fabric combinations you are using.

MATERIALS

Fabric Requirements

- yellow print: ¾ yd (68.6cm)
- blue print: ½ yd (45.7cm)
- green print: 1 yd (91.4cm)
- yellow plaid: ½ yd (45.7cm)
- pink plaid: ½ yd (45.7cm)
- green plaid: ½ yd (45.7cm)
- backing: 2⅞ yds (2.6m)
- batting: crib size or 51" × 60" (1.3m × 1.5m)

CUTTING DIRECTIONS

Materials	Cut	To Yield
yellow print	(5) 5" × 42" (12.7cm × 1m) strips	(10) 5" (12.7cm) squares
		(56) 2" × 5" (5.1cm × 12.7cm) rectangles
blue print	(3) 5" × 42" (12.7cm × 1m) strips	(10) 5" (12.7cm) squares
		(28) 2" × 5" (5.1cm × 12.7cm) rectangles
green print	(4) 5" × 42" (12.7cm × 1m) strips	(14) 5" (12.7cm) squares
	(6) 2¼" × 42" (5.7cm × 2m) binding strips	(26) 2" × 5" (5.1cm × 12.7cm) rectangles
each plaid	(7) 2" × 42" (5.1cm × 1m) strips	(20) 2" × 8" (5.1cm × 20.3cm) rectangles
		(20) 2" × 5" (5.1cm × 12.7cm) rectangles

Assembling the Blocks

1. Sew the 2" × 5" (5.1cm × 12.7cm) green plaid rectangles to 10 yellow 5" (12.7cm) squares. Press toward the plaid rectangles (Figure 1).

2. Repeat Step 1 with 10 blue squares and yellow plaid rectangles, and 10 green squares with pink plaid rectangles. Press toward the rectangles (Figure 2).

3. Sew the matching 2" × 8"(5.1cm × 20.3cm) plaid rectangles to the sides of each of the blocks. Press toward the long rectangles. Make 10 blocks of each color combination (Figure 3).

Figure 1   Figure 2

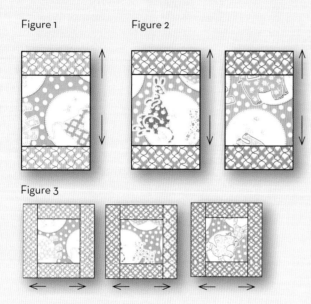

Figure 3

Assembling the Quilt

1. Arrange the blocks as shown or create your own arrangement. Rotate the blocks so the long rectangle in 1 block is next to the short rectangle in the adjoining block (no seams to match up!). Press toward the long rectangles (Figure 4).

2. Sew together 6 blue, 6 green and 13 yellow rectangles for the top border. Press the seams all in one direction. Sew to the top of the quilt. Press toward the quilt. Repeat for the bottom border (Figure 5).

3. Sew together 8 blue, 7 green and 15 yellow rectangles for the side border. Make 2. Press the seams all 1 direction. Add green corner squares at both ends of the borders. Press toward the squares. Sew to the sides of the quilt.

Note: The borders can be adjusted as needed by stitching random seams wider or narrower.

Figure 4

Figure 5

Finishing the Quilt

1. Layer, baste and quilt as desired. The quilt shown was machine stitched in the ditch around each of the center squares and between each block. The border was stitched in the ditch between the rectangles.

2. Baste a scant ¼" (6mm) from the edge of the quilt by hand or with a walking foot.

3. Join the binding strips with diagonal seams pressed open. Fold the binding in half, right sides together, and press to make a double binding. Match the raw edges of the binding to the edge of the quilt and stitch the binding in place, mitering the corners.

4. Trim the excess batting and backing evenly to ¼" (6mm). Turn the binding to the back side and stitch down by hand with matching thread.

Variation:
Sew-Easy Baby Quilt

For a completely different look, bright colors were used to frame a light print featuring owls. Any combination of fabrics will look great in this pattern—give it a try!

MATERIALS

fabric requirements

- white print: 1⅛ yds (1m)
- green, blue, pink and orange polka dots: ½ yd (45.7cm) each
- yellow daisy: 1 yd (91.4m)

CUTTING DIRECTIONS

Materials	Cut	To Yield
white print	(7) 5" × 42" (12.7cm × 1m) strips	(30) 5" squares (56) 2" × 5" (5.1cm strips × 12.7cm) rectangles
5 prints	(4) 2" × 42" (5.1cm × 1m) strips	(12) 2" × 8" (5.1cm strips × 20.3cm) rectangles
	(1) 5" × 42" (12.7cm × 1m) strip	(12) 2" × 5" (5.1cm strips × 12.7cm) rectangles
yellow daisy	(1) 5" × 42" (12.7cm × 1m) strip	(4) 5" (12.7cm) squares for corners
	(6) 2¼" × 42" (5.7cm × 1m) strips	binding

Twist and Shout

FINISHED DIMENSIONS: 21¼" × 25¼" (51CM × 64.1CM) BLOCK SIZE: 2¾" (7CM)

Pinwheel, Whirligig and Waterwheel are all names for the block used in this quilt. It's an interesting block, but we tend to avoid it because it involves using templates. I've eliminated the templates by strip piecing, then cutting triangles from the strips. There is a bit of waste with this method, but since the pieces are so small, it is worth the time it saves! You'll find this to be a quick and easy quilt.

MATERIALS

Fabric Requirements

- 1 yd (91.4cm) vintage white
- 6 fat quarters of assorted prints
- Fat quarter red check (binding)
- ¾ yd (68.6cm) backing
- 26" × 29" (66cm × 73.7cm) batting

CUTTING DIRECTIONS

Materials	Cut	To Yield
Vintage white	(10) 1¾" × 40" (4.4cm × 1m) strips (5) 1¼" × 40" (3.2cm × 1m) strips (6) 1¼" × 40" (3.2cm × 1m) strips	(30) 1¾" × 13" (4.4cm × 33cm) strips for blocks (49) 1¼" × 3¼" (3.2cm × 8.3cm) sashes Inside and outside borders
From each of six fat quarter prints	(5) 1¾" × 20" (4.4cm × 50.8cm) strips (1) 1¼" × 20" (3.2cm × 50.8cm) strip	(5) 1¾" × 13" (4.4cm × 33cm) strips for blocks (4) 1¼" × 3¼" (3.2cm × 8.3cm) border segments (5) 1¼" (3.2cm) squares
Red check	2" (5.1cm) bias strips	Binding

Sew exact ¼" (6mm). Place fabrics right sides together for sewing, unless otherwise noted.

Block Assembly

(Make 30)

1. Sew 1¾" × 13" (4.4cm × 33cm) white and print strips together (Figure 1). Press the seam toward the darkest fabric. Cut each strip set into four 3" (7.6cm) squares (Figure 1), then cut each square once on the diagonal (Figure 2). Discard the triangles that are mostly white (Figure 3).

2. Sew 4 matching triangles together in pairs as shown (Figure 4). Press. Sew the pairs together. Twist the seam where it intersects to open it. Press. Refer to General Instructions for more instruction on this technique. Trim to 3¼" (8.3cm) square. Repeat to make 30 blocks (Figure 5).

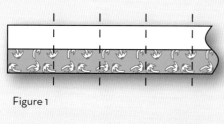

Figure 1

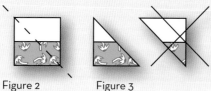

Figure 2   Figure 3

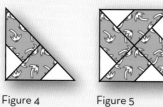

Figure 4   Figure 5
                  Make 30.

Assemble the Quilt

1. Join 5 blocks in a row with 4 white sashing strips. Press toward the sashing strips. Make 6 rows (Figure 6).

Figure 6
Make 6.

2. Sew together 5 horizontal sashing rows with 5 white sashing strips and 4 print squares. Press toward the sashing strips (Figure 7).

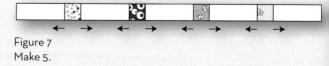

Figure 7
Make 5.

3. Join the block rows and the sashing rows, matching and pinning at each seam intersection. Press the rows toward the sashings.

Borders

1. Measure the quilt top through the middle of the quilt. Take this measurement and trim 2 white borders the width of the quilt. Sew to the quilt. Press toward the borders.

2. Measure the length of the quilt. Cut 2 white borders the length of the quilt. Sew to the quilt. Press toward the borders.

3. Piece together 5 print border segments alternated with 6 print squares to make a top border. Press (Figure 8).

4. Piece a similar border for the bottom of the quilt. Sew to the top and bottom of the quilt. Press toward the white border.

5. Piece together 6 border segments alternated with 9 squares for the sides of the quilt (2 segments at each end). Make 2 pieced borders. Sew to the quilt, pressing the seams toward the white border.

6. Measure, cut and sew the last white border to the top and bottom of the quilt. Measure, cut and sew the sides in the same manner. Press the seams toward the last border.

Quilting Suggestions

To prepare the quilt for quilting, layer the backing (which has been cut at least 4" [10.2cm] larger than the quilt top) wrong side up, followed by the batting (again, cut larger than the quilt top) and last, the quilt top, right side up. Thread or pin baste in a 4" (10.2cm) grid across the quilt. Quilt as desired.

The quilt shown was machine quilted in the ditch along the horizontal and vertical sashes and cornerstones, as well as on each side of the borders. An X was hand stitched through the middle of the blocks.

Binding

1. Before binding, hand baste a scant ¼" (6mm) from the edge of the quilt to prevent the layers from shifting.

2. Join the binding strips with diagonal seams pressed open. Press the binding in half lengthwise with wrong sides together.

3. Sew the binding to the quilt with a ¼" (6mm) seam allowance. Trim the excess batting and backing.

4. Turn the binding to the backside and stitch down by hand with matching thread.

5. Sign and date your quilt.

Figure 8

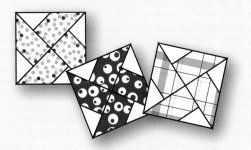

TIPS:

If the pieced borders don't fit exactly, you can take in or let out a few seams interspersed throughout the border.